RAINBOW BOA AS PET

The Ultimate Guide On Everything You Need To Know About Rainbow Boa As Pet

Thomas Bruce

Table of Contents

CHAPTER ONE

RAIN BOW BOA

Argentine rainbow boas (Epicrates Cenchria) are viewed as one of the more excellent snakes on the planet. In addition to the fact that they display dynamic orange and red tinge, however they additionally produce an inexhaustible measure of Rainbow radiances. Minute edges on their scales that refract light reason this wonder. Rainbow boas possess an enormous topographical range including South America and lower Central America.

RAINBOW BOA AVAILABILITY

Rainbow Boas are promptly accessible and can flourish in imprisonment with legitimate snake supplies, and cautious consideration regarding reptile wellbeing and health. They can be found at Exotic Pet stores, and at any neighborhood reptile appear.

Hereditary Mutations (Morphs) are accessible also, anyway they are extremely uncommon in

assortments and come bearing an enormous sticker price.

SIZE

Rainbow boas are conceived estimating around 8 to 12 inches. Grown-ups arrive at a normal length of 5 to 6 feet; Females will in general be somewhat bigger than guys in both size and length.

CHAPTER TWO

RAINBOW BOA LIFE SPAN

With the best possible consideration, hostage rainbow boas on normal live 20+ years. There have even been chronicles of females imitating at 24 years old years old.

With regards to Reptile Heating and Lighting for the Rainbow Boa, the perfect temperatures for rainbow boas are an evening time low of mid to low 70's Fahrenheit and a day time high in the low 80s F. High dampness is basic for Rainbow Boas. Day by day moistening ought to be utilized to keep up stickiness between 75-90 percent for grown-ups and 95 to 100 percent mugginess for neonates without the substrate being wet. A warm slope is additionally suggested. This is anything but difficult to accomplish by utilizing Zilla heat cushions, and additionally overhead lighting or snake heat lights, for example, the Solar Glo All in One Reptile Lamp, or brilliant warmth boards. Subspecies, for example, Brazilian rainbow (E.C. Cenchria) are progressively delicate to higher temperatures and ought to never be in delayed temperatures more than 90 F (except if being a gravid female). Colombian rainbow boas (E.C Maurus) will in general have a higher resistance for both higher daytime temperatures, and lower evening time temperatures, hence making this subspecies marginally simpler to keep than the Brazilian. I unequivocally prescribe utilizing an indoor regulator to direct appropriate temperatures, for example, a Zilla Terrarium Heat and Habitat Lighting Controller for Reptiles. By utilizing an indoor regulator you can guarantee that your fenced in area will never be excessively hot, or excessively cold, and has demonstrated to be a significant instrument to make ideal reproducing conditions.

The way to have your rainbow boa "shine" is light. A low wattage bright light mounted overhead will give a delightful rainbow show to your snake. Rainbow boas are essentially nighttime, so you will need to ensure your surrounding lights turn off for a night pattern of 8-12 hours utilizing Zoo Med's Repticare Day Night Reptile Timer. Encompassing lighting is likewise significant for any live plants you may use to enrich your terrarium.

CHAPTER THREE

RAINBOW BOA SUBSTRATE

The perfect snake bedding for rainbow boas is one that can withstand dampness without embellishment or separating. A portion of these substrates incorporate high evaluation reptile mulch, similar to cypress, coconut items, for example, Zoo Med's Eco Earth Loose Coco Fiber Substrate, and aquarium rock. Both sphagnum and green greenery are an incredible method to outwardly improve the appearance of your reptile terrarium, while giving additional dampness and expanding moistness. It is likewise essential to give a stow away to your rainbow boa Food.

Rainbow boas are commonly ravenous eaters getting a charge out of solidified or live reptile food. In the wild their eating regimen comprises of little well evolved creatures, rodents, winged creatures, bats, and even little reptiles including tegus (Tupinambis merianae). A variety in their hostage diet has not been demonstrated to be fundamental, and can get the job done on an all-rat diet.

Appropriate mugginess and accessible clean water is urgent for keeping a solid rainbow boa. Most rainbow boas flourish with moistness levels of 70 percent and higher, anyway Colombian rainbows (C.C.Maurus) are referred to flourish in dampness levels as low as 50 percent. Drying out and overheating are the two most normal reasons for mortality in rainbow boas. Indications of parchedness include: inadequate sheds, wrinkly dry scales, and spewing forth. A water source large enough for your snake to absorb is significant, and ought to be changed oftentimes to stay away from grimy stale water.

CHAPTER FOUR

RAINBOW BOA HANDLING AND TEMPERAMENT

Rainbow boas are commonly submissive and can withstand normal taking care of, anyway neonates (babies) will in general be somewhat nippy for the initial scarcely any months. This conduct is a characteristic sense for endurance, yet after a couple of suppers and some an ideal opportunity to conform to new environmental factors they appear to tame down and become incredible buddies.

Brazilian rainbow boas are nighttime, and they frequently become dynamic an hour or two after nightfall. They might be discovered scanning for a beverage or for another daytime concealing spot. When they have discovered an appropriate area, they accept a sit-and-hold up position with their heads reached out from their safe houses. Instead of effectively chasing down their prey, they likely search out high-rat traffic territories. When such a zone is discovered, they quietly hang tight for their next dinner.

The creator's Brazilian rainbow boa fenced in areas in this photograph each measure 36 inches in length by 24 inches wide by 21 inches tall.

Brazilian rainbow boas flourish in bondage and make superb pets as long as their prerequisites are met. The main interesting point is the pen. I have kept them in numerous sorts of walled in areas throughout the years. Plastic shoeboxes of different sizes, glass aquariums and exclusively fabricated wooden natural surroundings all do the trick. Whatever you use, it ought to be of suitable size and escapeproof. Fitting floor measurements for child Brazilian rainbow boas extend from plastic shoeboxes estimating around 12 inches in length by 6 inches wide by 4 inches tall to 10-gallon glass aquariums estimating 20 inches in length by 10 inches wide by 13 inches tall. It has been my experience that anything bigger than this is simply too enormous for a little snake. The temperature run all through a too-huge pen turns out to be unreasonably wide for the creature to thermoregulate.

When the snakes are around 2 feet in length, I move them to bigger plastic sweaterboxes. I use sweaterboxes 23 inches in length by 16 inches wide by 6 inches tall. Brazilian rainbow boas that are 2 feet in length can likewise be serenely kept in 20-to 30-gallon aquariums.

When the creatures are 4 to 6 feet in length, I move them into their grown-up fenced in areas. These are specially fabricated wooden pens. They are fixed within with Formica brand overlay to rise up to mileage from the snakes, dampness and cleaning. Grown-up confines are at least 36 inches in length by 24 inches wide by 21 inches tall. This size is suitable for lodging one creature or a rearing pair.

CHAPTER FIVE

CONCLUSION

Despite the size of the confine or the age of the snake, I generally organize within a similar way. A water dish is set in the cool finish of the confine away from the warmth source. In the warm finish of the confine, in any event one concealing spot is given. On the off chance that the confine is enormous or shared by numerous creatures, a few concealing spots are incorporated. Numerous things function as conceal spots: wooden or Rubbermaid encloses with openings the side, bits of broken ceramics, plug bark, record propped on blocks, and even ash squares laid on their sides. The snakes appear to love to wedge into the gaps of the ash squares.

Whatever things you use, ensure the shroud spots are satisfying to the eye, simple to evacuate for cleaning and organized so that they can't topple over and hurt the creatures. Rainbow boas will in general stay covered up during the day and appear to feel increasingly good on the off chance that they can escape sight.

HANDLE FREQUENTLY

Infant rainbow boas are cautious. This is reasonable in light of the fact that anything that may get them in the wild is most likely going to eat them. They should be taken care of normally to tame them. When your snake has adjusted to its new home and has all the earmarks of being eating consistently, don't hesitate to deal with it every now and again. Contingent upon the size of the feast they have as of late eaten, give them 24 to 72 hours to process before taking care of. Extremely, the more you pause, the better. Envision being gotten and moved around not long after you have eaten a huge supper. This can prompt spewing forth. With steady, delicate taking care of, child Brazilians tame down very quickly.

Like my rainbow boas' confines, their substrate changes with the size of the snake. Infants are kept on paper or paper towel. These are both simple to supplant when cleaning. Grown-ups are kept on enlivening western bark mulch from Earthgro. Its ruddy earthy colored shading gives it a characteristic look. Numerous things work to line your snake's pen. Consider appearance and simplicity of cleaning when settling on your decision. Similarly as with most reptiles, it is imperative to abstain from utilizing cedar or redwood shavings on the grounds that these contain synthetic concoctions poisonous to snakes.

THE END